UPDATED EDITION

Guess What!

Pupil's Book 2
with eBook

British English

Susannah Reed with **Kay Bentley**
Series Editor: Lesley Koustaff

CAMBRIDGE

Contents

Hello again!

Look!

Guess What!

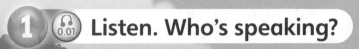

1 🎧 0.01 **Listen. Who's speaking?**

2 🎧 0.02 **Listen, point and say.**

1 Ben
2 Olivia
3 David
4 Tina
5 Leo

3 🎧 0.03 **Listen and find.**

Find Leo

Say the chant.

sister

This is my sister.
Her name's Olivia.
How old is she?
She's eight.

brother

friend

friend

 Find the mistakes and say.

Number 1. His name's
Ben. He's eight.

1

Name:
David
Age:
6

2
Name:
Tina
Age:
7

3

Name:
Ben
Age:
5

4

Name:
Olivia
Age:
9

→ Activity Book page 5

Vocabulary **7**

6 🎧 0.06 **Sing the song.**

Happy, happy, look and see,
We can sing our ABC.

7 🎧 0.07 **Listen and point.**

Dan   Jill   Sam   Sue   Tom

8 (About Me) **Ask and answer.**

What's your name?   My name's Harry.

How do you spell Harry?   It's H-A-R-R-Y.

 Grammar fun! ▶

8

Grammar: *Hello. What's your name?*
How do you spell … ?

→ Activity Book page 6

9 🎧 0.09 Listen, look and say.

1 What's this?

It's a ruler.

2 What are these?

They're books.

10 🎧 0.10 Listen and point.

1 **2** **3**

a **b**

11 Ask and answer.

B, 2. What's this?

It's a red bike.

→ Activity Book page 7

Grammar: *What's this?*

Grammar fun!

13 **Talk Time** **Listen and act.**

Animal sounds

14 **Listen and say.**

The rabbit can run. The lion is lazy!

What type of **art** is it?

1 0.16 **Listen and say.**

photography   drawing   sculpture   painting

2 CLIL **Watch the video.**

3 **Look and say the type of art.**

Number 1. Sculpture.   Yes.

Guess What!

Let's collaborate!

ARE WE THE SAME?

compare   discuss

think   ask   talk

answer

1 Transport

Look!

Guess What!

15

1 🎧 **1.01** Listen. Who's speaking?

2 🎧 **1.02** Listen, point and say.

1 plane

2 helicopter

3 bus

4 car

5 lorry

6 motorbike

7 train

8 boat

9 tractor

3 🎧 **1.03** Listen and find.

Find Leo

→ Activity Book page 12

4 🎧 1.04 Say the chant.

car

This is my car.
It's a big, red car.
This is my car,
And it goes like this.
Vroom! Vroom!

bike

train

boat

5 Match and say.

Number 1, c. It's a tractor!

1
2
3
4

a
b
c
d

6 About Me Ask and answer.

Do you like motorbikes?   Yes, I do.

7 **Sing the song.**

I've got a  ,
You've got a .
He's got a ,
She's got a .

Let's play together.
Let's share our toys.
Let's play together.
All the girls and boys.

I've got a ,
You've got a .
He's got a ,
She's got a .

Let's play together ...

I've got a ,
You've got a .
He's got a ,
And she's got a .

Let's play together ...

8  **Listen and say the name.**   She's got a train.   May.

Tim   May   Alex   Lucy

 Grammar fun!

Grammar: *I've got a lorry.*   → Activity Book page 14

9 **Listen, look and say.**

Has he got a plane?

Yes, he has.

Has she got a plane?

No, she hasn't. She's got a car.

10 🎧 1.10 **Look and match. Then listen and answer.**

Number 1. Has she got a ball?

No, she hasn't.

11 **Ask and answer.**

Number 1. Has she got a ball?

No, she hasn't.

Grammar: *Has he got a plane?*

Grammar fun!

1 Ben's got a helicopter!

Let's go to the park!

2 Has Ben got a robot?

No, he hasn't. It's a helicopter.

3 Can I have a turn, please?

Yes, of course!

4 Thank you. This is fun!

Be careful, iPal!

5 Sorry. Now let's play with my helicopter!

It's OK.

6 Wow! The helicopter is iPal!

13   **Listen and act.**

Animal sounds

14  **Listen and say.**

A gorilla in the garden. A hippo in the house.

Where is the transport?

1 🎧 1.16 Listen and say.

on land

on water

in the air

2 CLIL ▶ Watch the video.

3 Look and say *on land*, *on water* or *in the air*.

Number 1. On land.   Yes.

Guess What!

Let's collaborate!

OUR ECO-FRIENDLY TRANSPORT

draw   ferry

invent   choose   bike   car

→ Activity Book page 18   CLIL: Science   23

2 Pets

Guess What!

25

1 🎧 2.01 **Listen. Who's speaking?**

2 🎧 2.02 **Listen, point and say.**

1 woman

2 man

Pet Show

3 girl

4 cat

5 mouse

6 fish

7 boy

8 dog

9 baby

10 frog

Find Leo

3 🎧 2.03 **Listen and find.**

→ Activity Book page 20

4 2.04 Say the chant.

mice

fish

One frog, two frogs.
Big and small.
Come on now, let's count them all.
One, two, three.
Three green frogs.

dogs

frogs

5 Look, find and count.

I can see two women.

women

men

babies

children

6 About Me Your classroom. Look and say.

I can see five boys.

7 (2.06) **Listen, look and say.**

1 beautiful

2 ugly

3 old

4 young

5 happy

6 sad

7 big

8 small

8 (2.07) **Listen, find and say.**

They're cats.

They're happy.

9 **Make sentences. Say *yes* or *no*.**

Number 1. It's a bird. It's ugly.

No. It's beautiful.

Grammar: *It's beautiful.*

→ Activity Book page 22

10 🎧 2.08 Sing the song.

I'm at the pet shop.
I'm at the pet shop.
Can you guess which is
my favourite pet?

Is it small? No, it isn't.
Is it big? Yes, it is.
Is it beautiful? No, it isn't.
Is it ugly? Yes, it is.
It's big and ugly.
Let me guess, let me
  guess – oh yes!
It's a fish! It's a fish!

I'm at the pet shop.
I'm at the pet shop.
Can you guess which
are my favourite pets?

Are they old? No, they aren't.
Are they young? Yes, they are.
Are they sad? No, they aren't.
Are they happy? Yes, they are.
They're young and happy.
Let me guess, let me guess – oh yes!
They're dogs! They're dogs!

11 Think Play the game.

Is it happy?   No, it isn't.

Is it a dog?   Yes, it is!

Are they beautiful?   No, they aren't.

Are they spiders?   Yes, they are!

1. Look! What's that?
   It's a frog!

2. It's Aunt Sue! Hello.
   Oh dear! She's sad.

3. Can we help?
   Yes, please. I can't find my cat.
   MISSING

4. Mr Tom. He's big … and he's beautiful!
   What's his name?
   MISSING

5. What's that?

6. Thank you.
   You're welcome!

Value: Be helpful

→ Activity Book page 24

13 **Talk Time** Listen and act.

Animal sounds

14 (2.13) Listen and say.

A **f**ox with a **f**ish. A **v**ulture with **v**egetables.

What do animals need?

1 🎧 2.15 Listen and say.

water

food

shelter

2 CLIL ▶ Watch the video.

3 Look and say *water*, *food* or *shelter*.

Number 1. Water.   Yes!

Guess! What!

Let's collaborate!

OUR PET VIDEO

find out

think

choose

film

discuss

agree

Review Units 1 and 2

1 Look and say the word. Number 1. Bus.

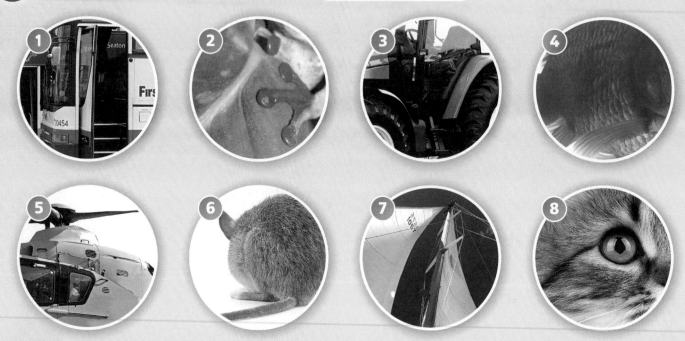

2 🎧 2.16 Listen and say the colour.

Tony   Anna   May   Bill

→ Activity Book pages 28–29

3 Play the game.

What's this? / What are these?	How do you spell ...?	What has he/she got?	Is he / Are they ...?
1	2	3	4

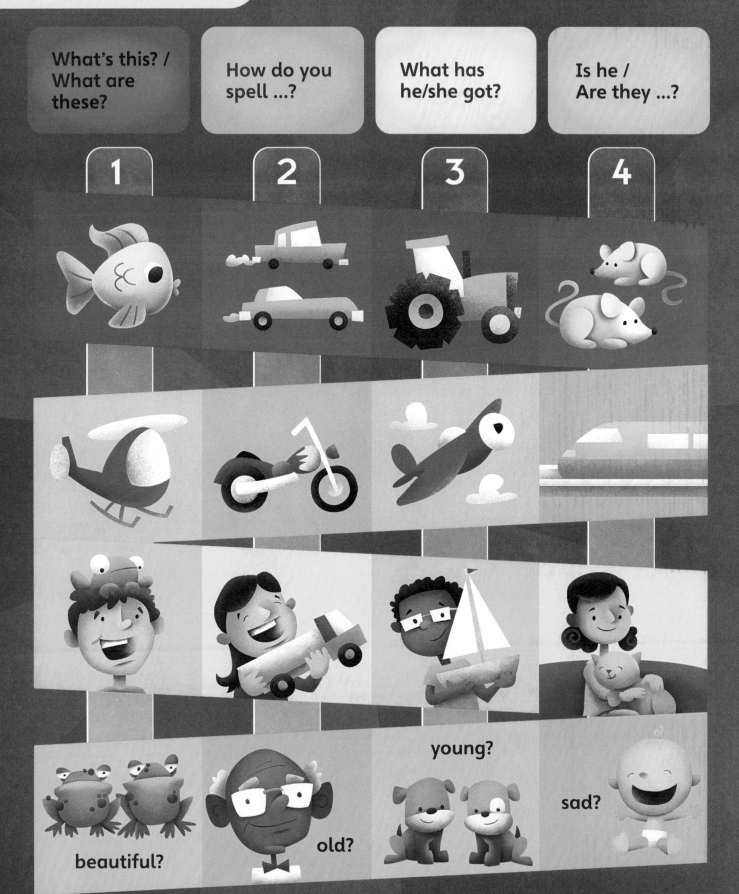

young?

beautiful?   old?   sad?

3 Clothes

Look!

Guess What!

37

1 3.01 Listen. Who's speaking?

2 3.02 Listen, point and say.

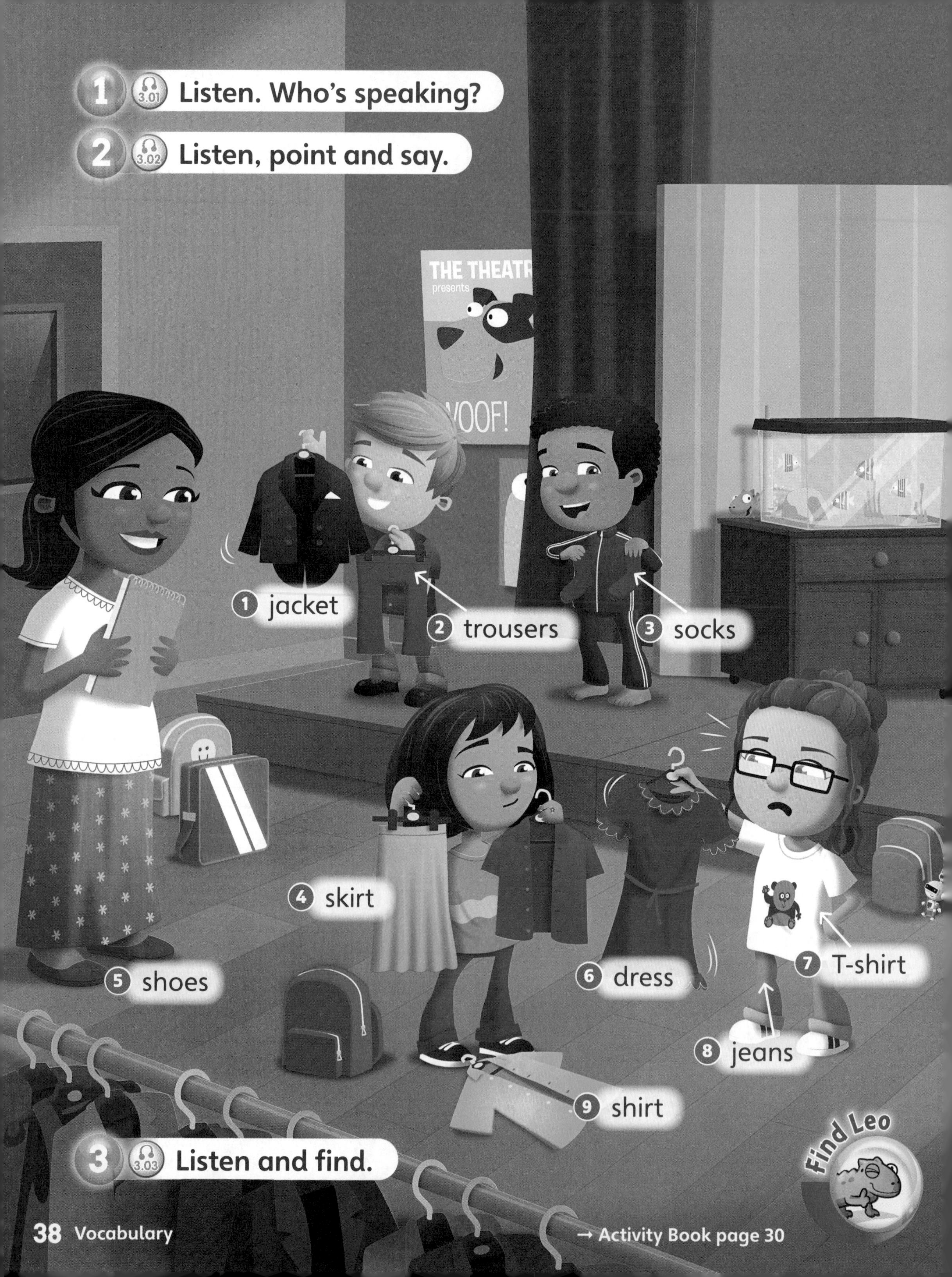

THE THEATR
presents
1 jacket
2 trousers
3 socks
4 skirt
5 shoes
6 dress
7 T-shirt
8 jeans
9 shirt
Find Leo

3 3.03 Listen and find.

→ Activity Book page 30

4 3.04 **Say the chant.**

red jacket

green T-shirt

purple shoes

blue trousers

Here's your jacket,
Your favourite red jacket.
Put on your jacket,
Let's go out and play.

Here are your shoes,
Your favourite purple shoes.
Put on your shoes,
Let's go out and play.

5 Think **Find the mistakes and say.**

His T-shirt isn't red. It's yellow.

Her shoes aren't orange. They're red.

→ Activity Book page 31

6 (3.06) **Sing the song.**

What are you wearing?
What are you wearing?
What are you wearing today?

I'm wearing red ,
And a green .
I'm wearing a blue ,
And a yellow .
Oh! I look great today!

I'm wearing blue ,
And an orange ,
I'm wearing a green .
And a purple .
Oh! I look great today!

7 (3.07) (Think) **Listen and say the name.**

Sammy

Sally

8 (About Me) **Ask and answer.**

What are you wearing today?

I'm wearing a blue skirt.

Grammar: *What are you wearing?*   → Activity Book page 32

9 (3.08) **Listen, look and say.**

1 Are you wearing a blue T-shirt?

Yes, I am.

2 Are you wearing brown shoes?

No, I'm not.

10 (3.09) **Listen and point. Then play the game.**

Pink. Trousers.
Are you wearing pink trousers?

No, I'm not. My turn!

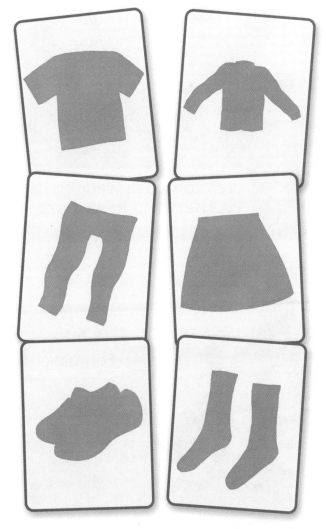

→ Activity Book page 33   Grammar: *Are you wearing a blue T-shirt?*

Grammar fun!

41

①

Look at these clothes!

Here's a hat for you!

②

What are you wearing?

They're clothes for a party!

③

A party?

Yes, look! I'm wearing big trousers and long shoes.

④

Here you are, iPal. You can use my hat.

Thank you.

And my jacket.

⑤

Look at me!

Fantastic!

⑥

First prize ... The robot!

Thanks. But I'm not a robot!

42 Value: Share things

→ Activity Book page 34

12 🎧 3.13 **Talk Time** Listen and act.

Animal sounds

13 🎧 3.14 Listen and say.

Jackals don't like jelly. Yaks don't like yoghurt.

→ Activity Book page 35   Functional language: *Here you are!*   Pronunciation: *j, y* **43**

What are
clothes
made of?

1 🎧 3.16 **Listen and say.**

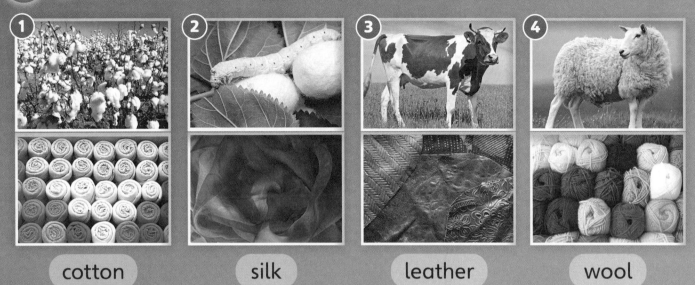

1 cotton

2 silk

3 leather

4 wool

2 CLIL ▶ **Watch the video.**

3 **Look and say the material.**

Number 1. Wool.   Yes!

Guess What!

Let's collaborate!

OUR **CLOTHES** COLLAGE

boots
jacket
agree
hat
create
design

→ Activity Book page 36

CLIL: Science

4 Rooms

Look!

Guess What!

theme

47

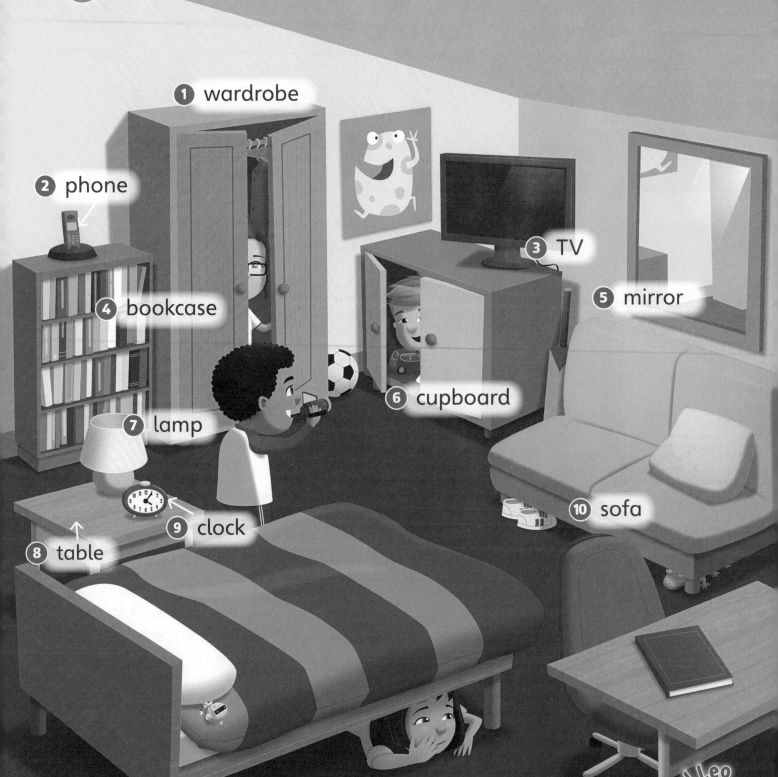

1 wardrobe

2 phone

3 TV

4 bookcase

5 mirror

6 cupboard

7 lamp

8 table

9 clock

10 sofa

Find Leo

3 (4.03) **Listen and find.**

Say the chant.

Is the lamp on the table?
Yes, it is. Yes, it is.
The lamp's on the table.

Are the books in the bookcase?
Yes, they are. Yes, they are.
The books are in the bookcase.

lamp

bookcase

clock

wardrobe

  Look, ask and answer.

Is the phone on the bookcase?

No, it isn't. It's on the table.

1

2 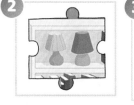 **3**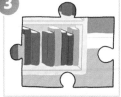

4

  What's in your bedroom? Think and say.

My computer is on my desk.

7 (4.06) **Sing the song.**

It's moving day, it's moving day
And everything's wrong on
moving day.

There's a  in the bathroom.
There's a in the hall.
There's a in the kitchen.
And I can't find my ball!

It's moving day …

There are four s in the garden.
There are two s on my bed.
There are three s on the sofa.
And where is baby Fred?

It's moving day …

8 (4.07) **Listen and say *yes* or *no*.**

Grammar: *There's a sofa in the bathroom.*   → Activity Book page 40

9  **Listen, look and say.**

10 **Listen, count and answer the questions.**

How many fish are there?

Seventeen!

11 (Think) **Play the game.**

There are three spiders.   No!

→ Activity Book page 41   Grammar: *How many books are there?*

51

Value: Be tidy

→ Activity Book page 42

13   (4.12) **Talk Time** **Listen and act.**

Animal sounds

14 (4.13) **Listen and say.**

Meerkats have got mouths. Newts have got noses.

How **many** are there?

1 (4.15) **Listen and say.**

lamppost   bus stop   letterbox   traffic light

2 CLIL ▶ **Watch the video.**

3 **Look and say the number.**

How many lampposts are there?

There are fourteen.

Guess What!

Let's collaborate!

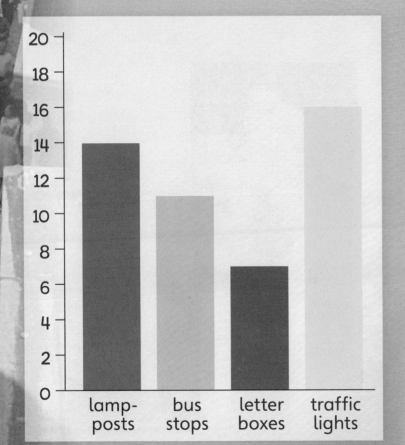

OUR **BAR CHART**

dining hall

classroom

library   office

count

compare

→ Activity Book page 44   CLIL: Maths

Review Units 3 and 4

1 Look and say the words.

Number 1. Jeans.

2 (4.16) Listen and say the colour.

3 Play the game.

Finish

Are you wearing a ? **17**

How many are there in your house? **18**

Are you wearing a  ? **19**

GO BACK ONE! **20**

MISS A TURN! **16**

How many  are there in your bathroom? **15**

Are you wearing a  ? **14**

How many  are there in your classroom? **13**

Are you wearing a  ? **9**

How many  are there in your kitchen? **10**

Are you wearing  ? **11**

GO BACK ONE! **12**

GO FORWARD ONE! **8**

How many  are there in your living room? **7**

Are you wearing  ? **6**

How many  are there in your bedroom? **5**

Are you wearing  ? **1**

How many  are there in your classroom? **2**

Are you wearing a  ? **3**

MISS A TURN!

Start

5 Meals

Look!

Guess What!

59

1 🎧 5.01 Listen. Who's speaking?

2 🎧 5.02 Listen, point and say.

The Caf
Breakfast 8-1
Lunch 12-3
Dinner 4-

3.65

1 potatoes
2 carrots
3 rice
4 peas
5 sausages
6 fish
7 meat
8 beans
9 toast
10 cereal

Find Leo

3 🎧 5.03 Listen and find.

→ Activity Book page 48

4 5.04 **Say the chant.**

breakfast

Do you like toast for breakfast?
Do you like cereal, too?
Toast and cereal for breakfast?
Yum! Yes, I do.

lunch

dinner

 5 Think **Read, look and say. What's missing?**

Shopping list

cereal

sausages

meat

peas

potatoes

beans

rice

fish

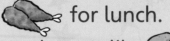

My friend Sammy likes
🍗 for lunch.
He doesn't like 🥔,
And he doesn't like 🫘.
He likes 🫘 and 🥕
And he likes 🧀.

Munch, Sammy.
Munch your lunch!

My friend Sally likes
🐟 for lunch.
She doesn't like 🧀,
And she doesn't like 🍗.
She likes 🫘 and 🥕
And 🥔 and 🫘.

Munch, Sally.
Munch your lunch!

7  **Listen and say *Sammy* or *Sally*.**

8 **(About Me)** **Ask and answer. Then say.**

Do you like fish?

Yes, I do.

Alex likes fish.

9 🎧 5.09 Listen, look and say.

1

2

10 Think Ask and answer.

Kim

Tony

Is it a boy or a girl?

It's a boy.

Does he like meat?

Yes, he does.

Does he like carrots?

No, he doesn't.

It's Tony!

Tom

Pat

→ Activity Book page 51   Grammar: *Does he like cereal?*

1

Look! Café Hawaii!

Café Hawaii

Let's go for lunch!

2 **Café Hawaii**

Would you like fish and potatoes?

Yes, please!

No, thank you!

3

What about carrots or peas, iPal?

No, thank you!

4

Oh dear! What would you like, iPal?

Cake! I like chocolate cake.

5

More cake, please!

No, iPal. That's enough!

6

What's the matter?

He likes chocolate cake – a lot!

12   **Listen and act.**

Animal sounds

13 🎧 5.13 **Listen and say.**

A seal in the sun. A zebra in the zoo.

What type of **food** is it?

1 🎧 5.15 Listen and say.

fruit　　**vegetables**　　**meat**　　**grains**　　**dairy**

2 CLIL ▶ Watch the video.

Guess What!

3 Look and say what type of food it is.

Number 1. Fish.　　Yes.

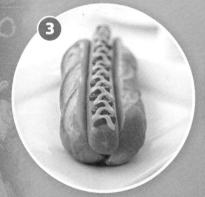 

Let's collaborate!

OUR NEW
HEALTHY
CAFÉ
MENU

lunch　discuss　dinner
breakfast　present
create

6 Activities

Look!

Guess What!

1 🎧 6.01 **Listen. Who's speaking?**

2 🎧 6.02 **Listen, point and say.**

Activity Day
What can you do?

1. play tennis
2. play hockey
3. play basketball
4. rollerskate
5. play baseball
6. ride a horse
7. fly a kite
8. take photos

TODAY!

3 🎧 6.03 **Listen and find.**

Find Leo

4 **Say the chant.**

I can play tennis.
I can't play hockey.
Let's play tennis.
Good idea!

basketball
baseball

fly a kite
ride a horse

take photos
rollerskate

5 **Match and say.**

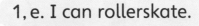 1, e. I can rollerskate.

1 I can rollerskate.
2 I can take photos.
3 I can ride a horse.
4 I can play tennis.
5 I can play hockey.

a

b

c

d

e

6 **Point and tell your friend.**

Picture b. I can play tennis.

Picture e. I can't rollerskate.

→ Activity Book page 57

7 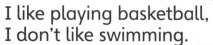 **Listen, look and say.**

1

> I like playing basketball, I don't like swimming.

2

> I like swimming. I don't like playing basketball.

8 (6.07) **Listen and say the name.**

Ann

Pam

Jack

Bill

Alex

Grace

9 (About Me) **Things you like. Think and say.**

> I like painting.

> He likes painting.

10 (6.08) Sing the song.

Do you like 🪁 ?
No, I don't. No, I don't.
Do you like 🚲 ?
Yes, I do. Yes, I do.
I like 🚲 !

Does he like 🪁 ?
No, he doesn't. No, he doesn't.
Does he like 🚲 ?
Yes, he does. Yes, he does.
He likes 🚲 !

Do you like 🎾 ?
No, I don't. No, I don't.
Do you like ⚽ ?
Yes, I do. Yes, I do.
I like ⚽ !

Does she like 🎾 ?
No, she doesn't. No, she doesn't.
Does she like ⚽ ?
Yes, she does. Yes, she does.
She likes ⚽ !

11 (6.09) Think Listen and say the number.

1

2

3

4

5

6

1. It's a basketball!

Are you OK, David?

2. The All Stars are my favourite team!

Let's play! Put on these shirts!

3. HOME GUEST

That's not fair!

Play nicely, iPal.

4. I'm sorry.

That's OK.

5. HOME GUEST

Watch me! Throw the ball like this.

Yes!

6. HOME GUEST

Well done, Olivia!

Thanks, iPal.

Value: Play nicely

→ Activity Book page 60

13   **Talk Time** **Listen and act.**

Animal sounds

14 **Listen and say.**

A camel with a camera. A kangaroo with a kite.

What **equipment** do we need?

1 🎧 6.15 Listen and say.

rackets   sticks   bats   balls

2 CLIL ▶ Watch the video.

3 Look and say *racket*, *stick*, *bat* or *ball*.

Number 1. Ball.   Yes!

Guess What!

Let's collaborate!

LET'S EXPLAIN A GAME

actions   agree   present   body parts   team   find out

Review Units 5 and 6

 Look and say the words. Number 1. Fly a kite.

2 **Listen and say the colour.**

Sue

Dan

→ Activity Book pages 64–65

3 Play the game.

7 In town

Look!

Guess What!

81

1 🎧 7.01 **Listen. Who's speaking?**

2 🎧 7.02 **Listen, point and say.**

1 park

2 cinema

CINEMA

Now Showing: **Robots From Outer Space**

3 clothes shop

The Clothing Store

4 café

Cozy Café

5 toy shop

The Toy Shop

6 book shop

Bert's Books

7 supermarket

Supermarket

Beans Get 1 Free

Coffee 30% Off

Fruit & Ve

8 street

SCHOOL

9 school

10 playground

Find Leo

3 🎧 7.03 **Listen and find.**

Say the chant.

Come with me and look around.
Who's in the café in the town?
It's my sister! She's in the café.
She's in the café in the town.

sister

brother

mum

dad

5 **Match and say.**   1, c. My cousin's in the playground.

1 My cousin's in the playground.
2 My aunt's in the clothes shop.
3 My uncle's in the school.
4 My grandma's in the supermarket.
5 My grandpa's in the park.

6 **Think of a place. Say and guess.**

There's a desk and green chairs.

It's a school.

7 🎧 7.06 **Sing the song.**

Come and visit my town,
My friendly little town.
It's nice to be in my town,
My little town.

There's a toy shop and
  a clothes shop.
There's a book shop
  and a cinema.
There's a café and
  there's
a supermarket.
In my little town.

And the toy shop is behind the
  clothes shop.
And the book shop is in front of
  the clothes shop.
And the clothes shop is between
  the book shop and the toy shop!
In my little town.

And the cinema is next to the café.
And the café is next to the supermarket.
And the café is between the supermarket
  and the cinema.

Come and visit my town …

8 🎧 7.07 **Look, listen and find the mistakes.**

The cinema is next
to the supermarket.

No it isn't. The cinema
is next to the café.

Grammar fun!

Grammar: *The toy shop is behind the clothes shop.* → Activity Book page 68

9 **Listen, look and say.**

Is there a playground behind the school?   Yes, there is.

Is there a café next to the cinema?   No, there isn't.

10 **Listen and say *yes* or *no*.**

11 **Play the game.**

Is there a café in front of the supermarket?

Yes, there is.

The cinema is next to the school.

No, it isn't. The cinema is next to the supermarket.

1 Cinema tickets!

They're from my cousin, Anna!

2 CINEMA — SUPERMARKET

Where's the cinema?

It's next to the supermarket.

3 Let's go!

No, iPal! Be careful!

4 Look left and right.

It's safe now. Let's cross.

5 Oh, no! It's closed today!

NOW SHOWING — The Queen

Come with me!

6 It's a film about robots!

I like going to the cinema.

Listen and act.

Animal sounds

14 (7.13) **Listen and say.**

A quick queen bee. An ox with an x-ray.

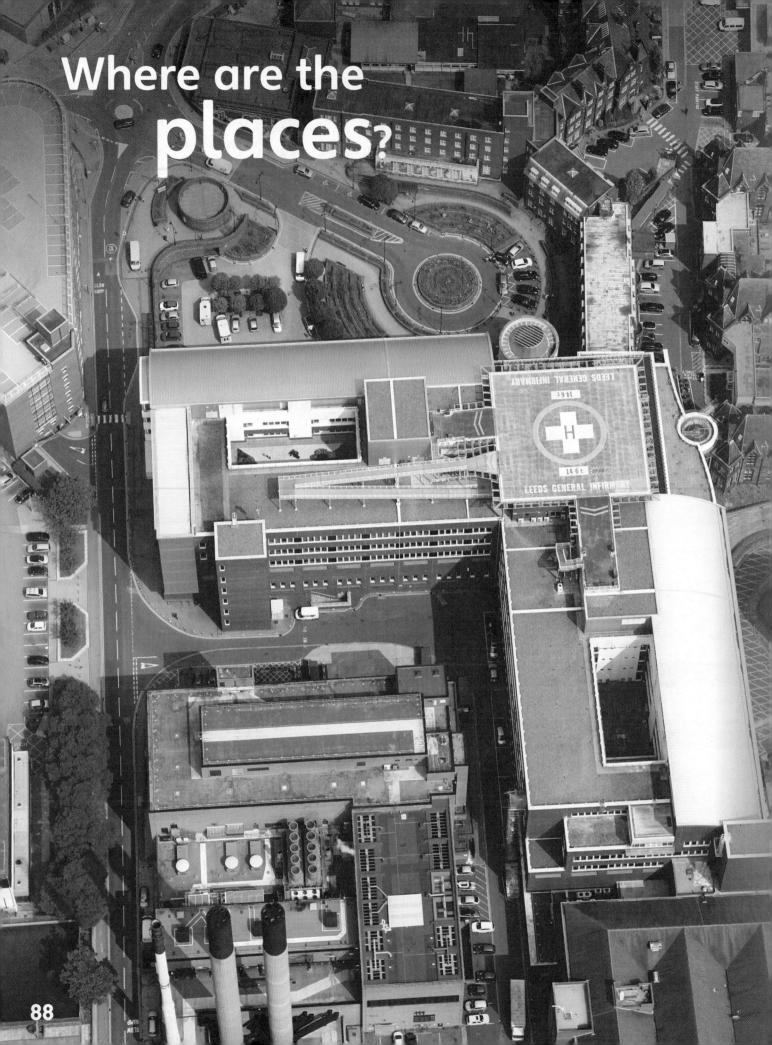

Where are the
places?

1 🎧 7.15 **Listen and say.**

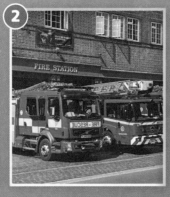

police station   fire station   hospital   sports centre

2 CLIL ▶ **Watch the video.**

3 **Look and say the letter and number.**

A, 3.   Fire station.   Yes!

Guess What!

Let's collaborate!

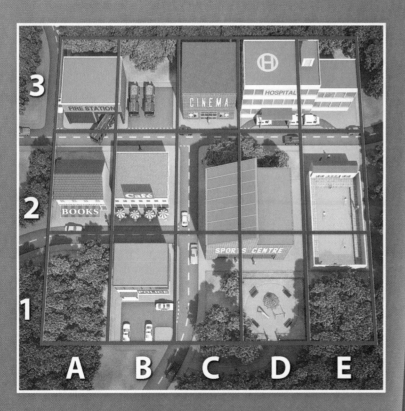

OUR IDEAL TOWN

make   park   draw   eco-friendly   bus stop   play

On the farm

Look!

▶

Guess What!

theme

1 🎧 8.01 Listen. Who's speaking?

2 🎧 8.02 Listen, point and say.

Café and Gift Shop

1 field

2 barn

3 horse

4 donkey

5 sheep

6 goat

7 cow

8 duck

3 🎧 8.03 Listen and find.

9 pond

Find Leo

4 🎧 8.04 Say the chant.

donkey

Where's the donkey?
It's in the barn.
It's in the barn.
On the farm.

Where are the goats?
They're in the field.
They're in the field.
On the farm.

cow

goats

ducks

5 Read and follow. Then ask and answer.

Where's the cow?   It's in the field.

a

1 Where's the cow?

2 Where are the ducks?

b

3 Where are the sheep?

4 Where's the horse?

c

6 About Me Ask and answer.

What's your favourite animal?   It's a sheep.

7 🎧 8.06 Sing the song.

Field and pond, house and barn,

Look at the animals on the farm …

What's the  doing?

It's swimming. It's swimming.

It's swimming.

What's the  doing?

It's swimming in the  .

Field and pond …

What's the 🐎 doing?

It's running. It's running. It's running.

What's the 🐎 doing?

It's running in the  .

Field and pond …

What's the 🐈 doing?

It's sleeping. It's sleeping.

It's sleeping.

What's the 🐈 doing?

It's sleeping in the 🏠 .

Field and pond …

What's the 🐄 doing?

It's eating. It's eating. It's eating.

What's the 🐄 doing?

It's eating in the 🛖 .

Field and pond …

8 🎧 8.07 Listen and answer the questions.

> What's the duck doing?

> It's swimming.

Grammar: *What's the duck doing?* → Activity Book page 76

9 (8.08) **Listen, look and say.**

1 Is the cat sleeping? Yes, it is.

2 Is the duck swimming? No, it isn't. It's flying.

10 (Think) **Play the game.**

Is the dog running?

Yes, it is.

Picture 1!

→ Activity Book page 77

Grammar: *Is the cat sleeping?*

Grammar fun!

🎧 8.10 **Story** ▶ **Listen and read. Watch.**

1 It's a message for iPal.

Let's find him!

2 Would you like to come to a party?

Yes, please!

3 Hold on!

We're flying!

4 Welcome to the party!

It's so nice to see you!

WELCOME HOME iP

5 What's Ben doing?

He's … dancing!

6 Goodbye, iPal!

Goodbye! Thanks for looking after me!

Value: Love your home

→ Activity Book page 78

12 **Talk Time** Listen and act.

Animal sounds

13 Listen and say.

A wolf in the water.
A white whale with a wheel.

Functional language: *Would you like to come to my party?*
Pronunciation: *w, wh* **97**

What do **farmers** do?

1 🎧 8.15 Listen and say.

plant seeds   turn soil   water plants   harvest plants

2 CLIL ▶ Watch the video.

3 Look and say.

Number 1. He turns the soil.   Yes!

Guess What!

Let's collaborate!

OUR **STORYBOARD** ABOUT LIFE ON **A FARM**

imagine

choose   discuss

find out   create

act out

Review Units 7 and 8

1 Look and say the words.

> Number 1. Café.

2 (8.16) Listen and say the name.

Grace

Lola

Kento

Dan

→ Activity Book pages 82–83

3 **Ask and answer.**

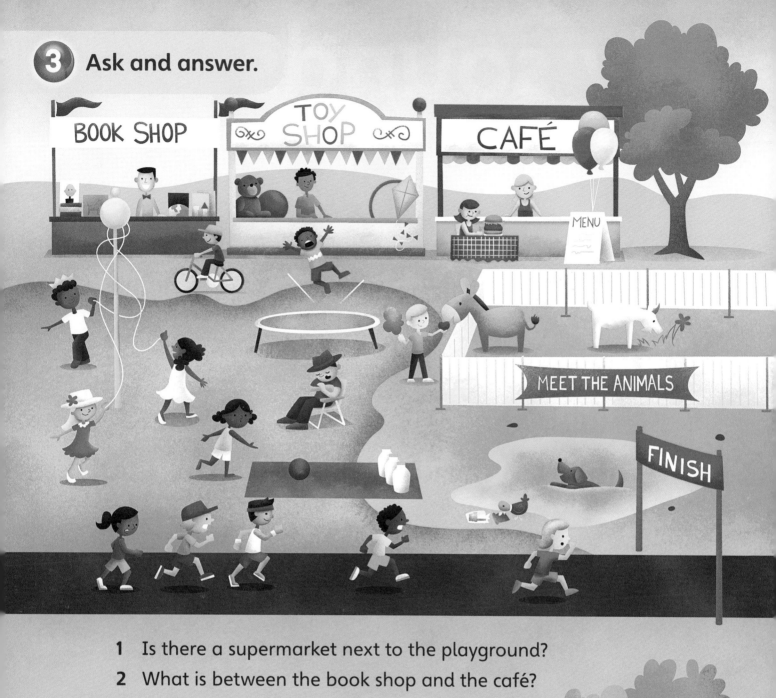

1   Is there a supermarket next to the playground?

2   What is between the book shop and the café?

3   Is there a pond in the park?

4   What is the duck doing?

5   Is the dog sleeping?

6   What is the donkey doing?

7   Is she eating cereal?

8   What's he doing?

9   Is she swimming?

10 What's he doing?

My sounds

lion • rabbit

gorilla • hippo

fox • vulture

jakal • yak

meerkat • newt

seal • zebra

camel • kangaroo

queen bee • ox

wolf • whale

Acknowledgements

Many thanks to everyone in the excellent team at Cambridge University Press & Assessment in Spain, the UK and India.

The authors and publishers would like to thank the following contributors:

Blooberry Design: concept design, cover design, book design
Hyphen: publishing management, page make-up
Ann Thomson: art direction
Gareth Boden: commissioned photography
Jon Barlow: commissioned photography
Ian Harker: class audio recording
Sounds like Mike Ltd: 'Grammar fun' recording
Robert Lee, Dib Dib Dub Studios: song and chant composition
Vince Cross: theme tune composition
James Richardson: arrangement of theme tune
Phaebus: 'CLIL' video production
Kiki Foster: 'Look!' video production
Bill Smith Group: 'Grammar fun' and story animations

The authors and publishers acknowledge the following sources of copyright material and are grateful for the permissions granted. While every effort has been made, it has not always been possible to identify the sources of all the material used, or to trace all copyright holders. If any omissions are brought to our notice, we will be happy to include the appropriate acknowledgements on reprinting and in the next update to the digital edition, as applicable.

Keys: U = Unit.

Photography

The following photos are sourced from Getty Images:

U0: Ariel Skelley/DigitalVision; enjoynz/DigitalVision Vectors; Corbis; enjoynz/DigitalVision Vectors; Sappington Todd/BLOOMimage; Burazin/The Image Bank; VISIT ROEMVANITCH; Burazin; Lane Oatey/Blue Jean Images; Lane Oatey/Blue Jean Images/blue jean images; Sappington Todd; aire images/Moment; Andrew Bret Wallis/Photodisc; Visit Roemvanitch/EyeEm; **U1:** Ayhan Altun/Moment; Aargentieri/iStock Getty Images Plus; szefei/iStock/Getty Images Plus; alxpin/E+; Henrik5000/E+; Spondylolithesis/E+; Klaus Vedfelt/DigitalVision; SteveDF/E+;CHUYN/DigitalVision Vectors; alxpin/E+; **U2:** antos777/iStock/Getty Images Plus; BarbarosKARAGULMEZ/iStock/Getty Images Plus; Aargentieri/iStock/Getty Images Plus; Lawrence Manning/Corbis; kgfoto/E+; Nophamon Yanyapong/EyeEm; Lew Robertson/Stone; Lényfotó pet photography/500px; RF Pictures/The Image Bank; Hans Surfer/Moment; Oscar Wong/Moment; Lucas Ninno/Moment; mehmettorlak/E+; dszc/E+; **U3:** hadynyah/E+; Emilia Drewniak/EyeEm; fotograzia/Moment; Santiago Urquijo/Moment; Sittichai Karimpard/EyeEm; Eduardo Lopez Coronado/EyeEm; Burazin/The Image Bank; Peter Dazeley/The Image Bank; Rawin Tanpin/EyeEm; Anatoliy Sadovskiy/EyeEm; mikroman6/Moment; kelly bowden/Moment; iStock/Getty Images; Eduardo1961/iStock; mikroman6/Getty images; Anatoliy Sadovskiy/EyeEm; **U4:** LeeYiuTung/iStock/Getty Images Plus; LianeM/iStock/Getty Images Plus; SDI Productions/E+; pepifoto/E+; Waridsara Pitakpon/EyeEm; Russ Witherington/EyeEm; Rizki Wanggono/EyeEm; **U5:** Andrew Olney/Stockbyte; Adam Gault/OJO Images ; bluehill75/E+; Mohd Haniff Abas/EyeEm; Stockbyte; FatCamera/E+; John A. Rizzo/Photodisc; Juanmonino/E+; AdShooter/E+; Mohd Haniff Abas /EyeEm; Stockbyte/Stockbyte; **U6:** Leander Baerenz/Getty Images ; Hybrid Images/Getty Images; Lauri Patterson/Getty Images; Image Source; Glyn Jones/Corbis/VCG; Yevgen Romanenko/Moment; Lawrence Manning/Corbis; Blake Little/Stone; George Doyle/Stockbyte; Photodisc; **U7:** lucentius/iStock/Getty Images Plus; Poh Kim Yeoh/EyeEm; MirageC/Moment; David Zaitz/The Image Bank Unreleased; Andersen Ross Photography Inc/DigitalVision; 500px Asia; LordRunar/E+; Nipitphon Na Chiangmai/EyeEm; Nipitphon Na Chiangmai/EyeEm; **U8:** BlazenImages/iStock/Getty Images Plus; Stephen Dorey/Getty Images; SCIENCE PHOTO LIBRARY; kickstand/E+; Burazin/The Image Bank; Life On White/Photodisc; Supawat Punnanon/EyeEm; Igor Alecsander/E+; Theerasak Tammachuen/EyeEm; Floortje/E+; Image Source.

The following photos are sourced from other source/libraries:

U0: VALUA VITALY; Jacek Chabraszewski; Monkey Business Images; BNP Design Studio; michaeljung; Anna Andersson Fotografi; terekhov igor; Wil Tilroe-Otte; Gena73; incamerastock/Alamy Stock Photo; Zoonar GmbH/Alamy Stock Photo; Robin Weaver/Alamy Stock Photo; REDPIXEL.PL; Yeamake; veryan dale/Alamy Stock Photo; Africa Studio/Shutterstock; Serge Vero/Shutterstock; Matej Kastelic; MaKars/Shutterstock; **U1:** James Steidl/Shutterstock; Margo Harrison; John Orsbun; Margo Harrison; James Steidl; Scott Rothstein;

one pony; s_oleg; Aprilphoto; Mikael Damkier; imageBROKER.com GmbH & Co. KG/Alamy Stock Photo; Buzz Pictures/Alamy; antb/Shutterstock ; Dhoxax/Shutterstock; Bailey-Cooper Photography/Alamy Stock Photo; David Fowler; Dwight Smith; Andrey Pavlov; Elena Elisseeva; Patrick Foto; maxpro; **U2:** Viorel Sima; stockyimages; StockLite; Gelpi; SurangaSL/Shutterstock; Barna Tanko; g215; Tierfotoagentur/Alamy; J Reineke; skynetphoto; Galyna Andrushko; Don Fink; Vitaly Titov; shane partdridge/Alamy; Mikael Damkier/Shutterstock; paul prescott/Shutterstock; Tsekhmister/Shutterstock; Olga Bogatyrenko/Shutterstock; DenisNata/Shutterstock; MANDY GODBEHEAR/Shutterstock; Judy Kennamer/Shutterstock; Monkey Business Images/Shutterstock; Willyam Bradberry/Shutterstock; Matthew Williams-Ellis/Shutterstock; Geoffrey Lawrence/Shutterstock; DreamBig/Shutterstock; **U3:** Mo Peerbacus/Alamy Stock Photo; Zoonar GmbH/Alamy; artproem/Shutterstock; Irina Rogova/Shutterstock; Tim Gainey/Alamy Stock Photo; Sofiaworld/Shutterstock; smereka/Shutterstock; Randy Rimland/Shutterstock; pixbox77/Shutterstock; Tramont_ana/Shutterstock; Derya Cakirsoy/Shutterstock; trossofoto/Shutterstock ; Anna Klepatckaya/Shutterstock; Picsfive/Shutterstock; karkas/Shutterstock; Gulgun Ozaktas/Shutterstock; Loskutnikov/Shutterstock; **U4:** donatas1205/Shutterstock; akud/Shutterstock; Image navi - QxQ images/Alamy Stock Photo; Justin Kase zsixz/Alamy; Design Pics/Alamy Stock Photo; Taina Sohlman/Shutterstock; ATGImages/Shutterstock; stocker1970/Shutterstock; Teerasak/Shutterstock; Kitch Bain/Shutterstock; Marek Ariel Skelley/DigitalVision Uszynski/Alamy; PearlBucknall/Alamy Stock Photo; Africa Studio/Shutterstock; Yeamake/Shutterstock; Nolte Lourens/Shutterstock; Image Source/Alamy; **U5:** Naho Yoshizawa/Shutterstock; Craig Richardson/Alamy; Tracy Whiteside/Alamy; Tetra Images,LLC/Alamy; Tracy Whiteside/Alamy; Stefano Politi Markovina/Alamy Stock Photo; matka_Wariatka/Shutterstock; Kolpakova Svetlana/Shutterstock; Jag_cz/Shutterstock; Christine Langer-Pueschel/Shutterstock; Christian Draghici/Shutterstock; koss13/Shutterstock; Christian Jung/Shutterstock; Africa Studio/Shutterstock; **U6:** Dan Thornberg/Shutterstock; Krakenimages.com/Shutterstock; Hurst Photo/Shutterstock; Alex White/Shutterstock; taelove7/Shutterstock; J.Helgason/Shutterstock; gorillaimages/Shutterstock; Veronica Louro/Shutterstock; Ramona Heim/Shutterstock; Rob Bouwman/Shutterstock; J. Helgason/Shutterstock; Production Perig/Shutterstock; Production Perig/Shutterstock; Phovoir/Shutterstock; ESB Professional/Shutterstock; Kuttig - People/Alamy; F1online digitale Bildagentur GmbH/Alamy; David Madison/DigitalVision; pukach/Shutterstock; anaken2012/Shutterstock; Image Source Plus/Alamy; Thyrymn2/Alamy; onilmilk/Shutterstock; Sean Gladwell/Shutterstock; Aaron Amat/Shutterstock; mexrix/Shutterstock; Pal2iyawit/Shutterstock; Ledo/Shutterstock; Nattika/Shutterstock; Ramon grosso dolarea/Shutterstock; Lotus_studio/Shutterstock; Bits And Splits/Shutterstock; Joe Gough/Shutterstock; Elnur/Shutterstock; Tracy Whiteside/Shutterstock; oliveromg/Shutterstock; Igor Dutina/Shutterstock; StockPhotosArt/Shutterstock; Leonid Shcheglov/Shutterstock.

Front Cover Photography

Front Cover Photo by Arthur Morris/Corbis Documentary.

Illustrations

Aphik; Andy Parker; Bill Bolton; Chris Jevons (Bright Agency); Joelle Dreidemy (Bright Agency); Gareth Conway; Kirsten Collier (Bright Agency); Marcus Cutler (Sylvie Poggio); Marek Jagucki; Phil Garner (Beehive Illustration); Richard Watson (Bright Agency); Woody Fox (Bright Agency).